CULTIVATE:

4 PRINCIPLES TO HELP YOUR MATE RECOGNIZE & FULFILL HER POTENTIAL

BY MAURICE ROGERS JR.

Dedication

To Kennedy, my wonderful daughter; I wrote these words with you in mind. May you find a true cultivator that seeks to help extract the gold hidden within you.

Contents

A special note to women readers

Although this book is primarily written as a guide for men; women are encouraged to enjoy it as well. Before we begin, I would like to answer a question that could arise upon reading the forthcoming pages.

Do you need a man to cultivate you?

In no way do you "need" a man to cultivate you. That would imply that you were defective in some way and the power to reach your potential was dependant on something outside of yourself. You are totally capable of defining and reaching your potential on your own. It is not a matter of ability, but of motivation and self-awareness.

This book is not a guide to how a man can give you value. It is a guide to how a man can make it easier for you to recognize your own. If you are single, or the man in your life is not being the cultivator you think he should be, listen to me very closely. You must take personal responsibility for identifying and manifesting your unique gifts and talents. Let nothing outside of you hold you back from recognizing and releasing the magnificence of what's inside you. Use this book as a guide to help you define your purpose, reassure you of your value, navigate the common pitfalls and achieve your potential.

The greatest good you can do for another is not just share your riches, but to reveal to him his own

— Benjamin Disraeli

The value of a woman

Women are precious gifts to the world; each with their own desires, perspectives and unique gifts. The tragedy is, these precious gifts often go unopened, never allowing themselves, or the world to truly see the magnificence of what's inside. Helping to extract this unexpressed treasure is what being a cultivator is all about. You don't give a woman value; she came to you packaged with it. A woman's inherent potential coupled with a man's sincere desire to help bring forth that potential can turn this world upside down. It's time for men to understand and fully operate in their role as cultivator.

Introduction

A man can be a woman's biggest liability or greatest asset. The fact that you are reading these words tells me you're probably the latter or would like to be. The willingness to humble yourself in order to seek knowledge above your own is a trait of an uncommon man. As you'll see in a coming chapter, this trait is invaluable to the growth of your mate and your relationship as a whole. Before we dive into the principles, let's set the context of this book by defining exactly what we mean by cultivate.

Cultivate defined

To cultivate is defined as:

1. To make better
2. To refine
3. To promote or improve the growth of, through labor and attention
4. To foster (to help something grow or develop)

As you can see, the word cultivate has to do with helping something become better through growth and development. You do this for your mate not by focusing on improving her, but by providing the environment in which she can naturally improve. Think of it as a fish in water or an animal in the wild. These animals are most comfortable and naturally thrive in their unique environments. You don't have to do much for them if their prescribed environments are intact and maintained. **This is the goal, challenge and responsibility of the cultivator: To develop and maintain an environment in which his mate's greatest self can grow**. This environment is a natural result of applying the principles we will discuss in this book. The principles are as follows:

- Principle #1 Uncover her purpose
- Principle #2 Encourage her
- Principle #3 Teach her
- Principle #4 Love her

The qualifications of a cultivator

What qualifies you to cultivate? A high ranking job? A perfect past? Money? Thankfully, none of the above. The only qualification of a cultivator is that you care. The desire to cultivate is the natural outpouring of caring. This idea frees you from the belief that your primary value to a relationship hinges on your material possessions. This is a disempowering concept that has left many good men feeling out of place and worthless. Material possessions come and go, but the heart of a cultivator is stable and true. Let your sense of value to the relationship stem from your role as cultivator; take pride in the fact that a caring heart is something money cannot buy.

Man to Man

I am no relationship expert. I don't write these words from a high-horse of perfection. Just like you, I am simply a man. Many of the lessons I will share with you are the products of pain. The pain of being misunderstood, the pain of broken promises and the pain of failed relationships. Never make the mistake of thinking a good man is a perfect man. Don't put that unrealistic pressure on yourself. A good man is one that pursues right. A good man is one that gets up when he falls. A good man is one that cultivates the best in himself and those around him.

CHAPTER 1

Principle #1
Uncover her purpose

> "To be what we are, and to become what we are capable of becoming, is the only end of life."
>
> — Robert Louis Stevenson

Who is your mate? Really, think about it. Who is she? Not her name, job title or family role. Who is she at her essence, her fundamental core? I would argue that if you don't know someone's purpose, you don't truly know them. The most authentic part of that individual is yet to be uncovered. We can know someone our entire lives and not truly "know" them. Life has its way of suffocating our true selves under a repetitious cycle of survival, family dynamics and crisis. This cycle has to be interrupted, and a new cycle initiated, one that shuns mediocrity and a life of basic maintenance; in favor of a pursuit of contribution, and authentic self-expression.

What is purpose?

The concept of purpose has been around for centuries. There are different schools of thought on what it means, how to describe it, and its origin. In an effort to keep things simple, let's describe purpose as authentic, more specifically, "the authentic use of something". Authentic is defined as: original, genuine, or accurate. This definition applies to everything created. Everything created has an original, genuine, or accurate use and is specifically designed to execute that use. For example, a car's most authentic use is to transport you from one place to another on the road; while an airplane's most authentic use is to transport you from one place to another through the air. The design and natural abilities of each creation reflects its different practical use.

How does this apply to your mate? Just like the car or airplane, she has a most authentic use. This "use" is a part of her very being; it is in line with her natural abilities, aptitudes and personality traits. **These unique endowments act as clues and indicators of what her purpose may be.**

Outer recognition vs. Inner recognition

The value of purpose is in the contribution it makes to the lives of others. Your ultimate goal is to help your mate recognize her inherent value and use that value to make the lives of others better. There are two steps in this process:

1. Outer recognition
2. Inner recognition

Outer recognition is when you identify the gift she has to give to the world through her purpose.

Inner recognition is when she recognizes and accepts the gift she has to give to the world through her purpose. Recognizing it means, she sees that it's there; accepting it means, she says yes to the invitation to demonstrate it in the world. Inner recognition is the most important step, but it is also the step you don't have complete control over. This entire book is a tool to help you ignite her inner recognition, but for now, let's focus on step 1.

Uncovering her purpose – Outer recognition

The answers to the following questions are clues to your mate's purpose. Some answers will immediately come to you, while others, you'll have to think about, or consult with her directly for more clarity.

1. What does she love to do and hate to stop doing?

2. What is she naturally gifted at doing? Communicating? Dancing? Listening? Teaching? Cooking? Leading others? Creating art?

3. What are her hobbies?

4. What is she the go-to expert for in her circle of family and friends?

5. What type of activities does she like to volunteer for?

6. What world problem consistently agitates her or makes her angry? Literacy? Poverty? Low-self esteem? Obesity? How the elderly are cared for? Racial injustice? The educational system?

7. If your family had all of your financial needs met, what type of job or service would she be perfectly content to provide for free? If you truly love something, you will do it with, or without, the promise of monetary gain. Although monetary compensation may be accepted, the primary compensation you receive from operating in your purpose is an inner sense of fulfillment and satisfaction.

8. What topics does she love to learn about?

9. What topics does she love to talk about?

10. Who are her heroes and why? Our heroes are usually people that exhibit qualities we would like to have, or stand for a cause we think is noble. For example, many of my personal heroes are teachers that made the world a better place with the power of their ideas. I admire these people because what they accomplished is in line with my purpose, and like me, her purpose may be closely linked to the people she admires.

At the heart of purpose is service. It's about identifying how you are best suited to make a difference in the lives of others. These questions are meant to help you discern your mate's purpose by defining her innermost passions, desires and natural inclinations. There will probably be a reoccurring theme in your answers, making it glaringly obvious what her purpose could be. If she seems to have many unrelated passions or desires, find out which one excites her most and begin there.

When documenting your answers, keep in mind that they must remain unique to her. You are not trying to manipulate, or mold her into your preferred idea of what she should be; you are trying to help her identify and bring forth her best self. Your goal is not to change her into something, but to help her become more of what she already is. The world doesn't need her to change; it needs her to show up empowered to be authentically and uniquely herself. This is where her true value, success and happiness lie.

Inner recognition

As I previously wrote, outer recognition is when *you* identify the gift she has to give to the world through her purpose. Inner recognition is when *she* recognizes and accepts that gift, and is ready to give it to the world through her purpose. Now that you have identified what you think her purpose may be, carefully present this information to her for confirmation. Express to her what you think her gifts and talents are and how they could possibly be used for good in the world. Get feedback on your thoughts, and most importantly, listen to what she thinks her gifts and talents are and how she sees herself using them to make a difference in the world. This is imperative because how she views herself, and what she believes she is capable of achieving, is the primary determinant in what she will actually achieve. Her level of fear, self-confidence, and current life priorities will all play a role in the response you will receive from her. A few of the most common reactions may be:

1. Confirmation

She recognizes her value, and is excited about moving forward with the application of her gifts. At this step, you and your mate essentially become partners in working toward reaching her full potential. This is the ideal state, and while it is possible, it is not something everyone should expect to achieve after their initial talk.

2. Overwhelmed

She may feel this was too much information all at once and may need time to think it over for discussion at a later date.

3. Disinterest

She may not fully grasp what you are communicating or simply may not want anything to do with it at this point.

Anything other than a favorable response may discourage you, but remember that a cultivator's primary role is not change, but to consistently provide an environment in which change can take place. With the correct environment in place (which will come as a result of applying the principles in this book) she is more likely to recognize the treasure she is, and begin to act as such in her own unique time.

■ Points to remember ■

1. Until you have uncovered your mate's purpose, you have yet to discover the most authentic part of her.

2. You don't decide your mate's purpose, you discern it.

3. Your mate's natural abilities, personality traits and aptitudes act as clues to what her purpose may be.

CHAPTER 2

Principle #2
Encourage her

"People go farther than they thought they
could when someone believes they can."
—John Maxwell

Encouragement is an essential element in achieving
one's potential. For this reason, the necessity of an
encouraging partner cannot be overstated. We are
affected most but what those closest to us say and do.
The sound of an encouraging voice provides a sense of
stability and confidence unmatched by anything else.
This principle is next in our journey because it picks
up where the last one left off. You have uncovered

your mate's purpose, now you must help draw it out through the power of encouragement.

4 Ways to encourage your mate

I define encouragement as any action that inspires positive change in someone. This can be manifested and applied in many different ways. The following are four practical ways you can encourage your mate. Each aimed at motivating her to take the first step, or go to the next level, in her purpose.

1.   Recognition

Recognition is affirming the distinguishing characteristics that make your mate different from others. We uncovered the raw material for this in the previous chapter. Depending on her unique gifts and talents this could mean affirming her entrepreneurial spirit, creativity, artistic skills, exceptional patience with children, or her empathy toward animal welfare. The keys are to always be sincere and specific. Others may trivialize or overlook her passions and unique gifts but your home must be a place where they are acknowledged and celebrated. Make a commitment to be your mate's most vocal supporter.

2.   Genuine interest

Genuine interest is an extremely gratifying form of encouragement. It communicates that the receiver and their work is important in the eyes of someone else. Show interest by:

- Inquiring about what her focus is at the moment, any challenges she may be facing, and if you could help in any way.
- Being a listening ear.
- Talking to her about her future goals and plans to achieve them.
- Periodically accompanying her to any events or rallies she may be interested in that are connected to her purpose.

I'll be the first to admit that this is not an easy task. It can be a challenge to consistently discuss a subject you may not particularly have a passion for yourself. Your interest must stem from its importance to her. It is important to her, so in turn, it must become reasonably important you. Your genuine interest is a vital form of encouragement.

3. Domestic support

Many men inadvertently overlook this method of encouragement; which can leave their mate feeling trapped and suffocated in their own home. The duties and expectations of being a lover, mother or housekeeper can become a prison to her purpose if not managed correctly. One of the ways you can help manage this dilemma is by consistently allotting time for her to do something pertaining to her purpose. Never forget that underneath her relationship and family roles is a unique individual with a purpose. This purpose needs, desires and deserves to be expressed. A true cultivator must be sensitive to this need and not neglect or downplay its importance.

4. Agitation

This is the form of encouragement that many great coaches use to bring the best out of their players. Initially, it isn't the most applauded, but in the end, the results are usually greatly appreciated. This approach is founded on a mixture of caring, recognition of potential, and expectations. Essentially, your job is to challenge, push and prod your mate to the next level in her development. Your voice of agitation will be a thorn in the side of comfort. For this, you will not always be liked, or responded to in a favorable manner. This reaction is usually temporary because over time, she will begin to understand what you're doing, and how it has helped her succeed in the past.

A word of caution; be sure not to make agitation the primary form of encouragement you employ. You will be perceived as overly critical and discouraging, leading to an atmosphere of demotivation instead of motivation. This is counter-productive, and could even prove to be detrimental to your relationship. I recommend a balanced use of all four methods; never completely relying on one, while neglecting to use the others.

3 Areas to focus your encouragement

There are three primary hindrances to your mate reaching her full potential. Some are easy to spot while others take a keen eye because they can disguise themselves as progress. Keep a close watch on these areas and make them the focal point of your encouragement.

1. Self-doubt

There is a silent epidemic in our society; one marked by low self-confidence and low self-worth. This self-depreciating philosophy is based on the erroneous belief that we are less valuable or capable than we actually are. It is not outwardly said, but is inwardly felt, and displayed in our daily actions.

We tend to undervalue what we are, and overvalue what we are not; magnifying the gifts and talents of others, while minimizing our own.

When you think less of yourself, you attempt less. The ceiling of what you can accomplish becomes restricted by your limiting self-belief. Low self-confidence is not a gender problem, it is a human problem; something that we all struggle with from time to time. Help your mate understand that she is just as valuable and capable as anyone else. Through the power of encouragement, we can draw strength from someone else's belief in us, when we're having trouble believing in ourselves.

2. Complacency

Complacency is a primary hindrance to fulfilled potential; it stems from a state of mental acceptance and contentment. This mental acceptance destroys your motivation and desire to reach for more. Contented people are comfortable people. Comfortable people don't reach for a better future. People that don't reach for a better future can never realize their full potential.

This cycle is commonly seen in the modern workplace; which I call, the graveyard of purpose. The workplace is a reservoir of unrealized dreams and goals, abandoned in the name of comfort. The only way to loosen the grip of comfort is to disrupt it with the encouragement of agitation (as discussed in the previous section).

Ask yourself these questions:

- Does your mate genuinely love her current job?
- Does it tap into her most authentic use?

- Are her gifts and talents being used and appreciated?
- Is she compromising her purpose for her paycheck?
- What *practical steps* could she take to get in a work environment more conducive to her purpose?
- Would she like to be a business owner? If so, what *practical steps* could she take toward forming her own business?

Comfort is a subtle, yet powerful enemy. Once you've adapted and settled into its grooves, it can be hard to get out. Be diligent, yet patient in the process of helping your mate break free from the chains of comfort.

3. Lack of consistent focus

The last major hindrance to your mate reaching her potential is lack of consistent focus. The success fundamentals of focus and consistency are different, yet so closely related, I group them together as one. Simply put, focus is choosing a point of concentration. Consistency is maintaining a point of concentration over an extended period of time. I find this to be a challenge for many women because of their instinctual ability to learn, adapt and succeed at many things. Unchecked, this seemingly harmless trait leads to a life of dabbling. Nothing will quite get her entire focus, leading to mediocrity in many things instead of greatness in one or two. A woman that does not know herself is cursed with being successful at the wrong thing. Since she is not anchored in place by purpose, she is open game to any fleeting desires or opportunities that come her way. Help protect her focus by measuring opportunities against how they contribute to her overall purpose.

Guard against unbelief

Many futures have been abandoned due to the unbelief of a mate. Often, you are the first to hear about a dream while in its most fragile state. Do not take this responsibility lightly. Your support, or lack thereof, can quite literally mean the life or death of a dream. This does not mean you need to support any impractical idea your mate thinks up. It means that you must take your role as a critical voice of encouragement very seriously and choose your response with care. Unbelief has a tone. Unbelief has a facial expression. Unbelief has a posture. Unbelief is poison. Guard against unbelief. It can abort the seed of a dream before it has time to mature.

▪ Points to remember ▪

1. Encouragement is an essential element in achieving one's potential.

2. A man should be his mate's most vocal encourager.

3. There are four primary ways to encourage your mate, each are of equal importance: recognition, genuine interest, domestic support, and agitation.

4. There are three primary hindrances to your mate reaching her potential: self-doubt, complacency, and lack of consistent focus.

CHAPTER 3

Principle #3
Teach her

"The greatest teacher is exemplification."
– Albert Einstein

The principle of teaching is of great importance. It is a privilege, as well as an immense responsibility of the cultivator. When you think of teaching, you probably think of the student-teacher relationship in a classroom. This teaching dynamic is different because neither of you functions as the sole authority; each are simply fellow travelers and partners on the road to expressing their individual potential.

Teaching is about thoroughly conveying an idea or message. Many people think of this as primarily being executed by auditory means. Although what you say is of great importance, it pales in comparison to what you do. This principle is about becoming more conscious of the specific message you send through your words, and most importantly, the actions that follow.

Your life message

You communicate to the people around you through your life conduct. The message your conduct sends is what I call your "life message". Among other things, you communicate what is important to you, how you handle adversity and what you truly believe about various aspects of life. This truth makes everyone a teacher, but most are oblivious to what they are teaching and the impact it has on others. Your actions speak louder and longer than what you say. The message you send through your life conduct is an integral component in forming an environment conducive to the positive growth of your mate.

Leading by doing

Throughout this book, our focus has been identifying the inherent potential in your mate, helping her recognize it, and removing the most common barriers to its achievement. As you support her, your life conduct should demonstrate that you recognize your own potential and are passionately in its pursuit. **A man visibly nonchalant regarding the expression of his individual potential creates a discrepancy in his affirmation of the potential of others.** However, a man whose actions match his affirmation of what is possible for others actively communicates believability and a feeling of inspiration that helps move them to action.

Let's take the lens off of your mate and focus it on you for a moment. The following are a few questions to help you think through your current life message. This self-introspective work is one of the key components of this book.

1. Do you have an idea of what your purpose is, and most importantly, are you actively pursuing it?

2. What is the biggest goal you're currently pursuing? Does your mate know what it is?

3. Are you sending a message through your actions that complacency is acceptable?

4. Are you a dabbler? Jumping from venture to venture without remaining focused and consistent on one thing over the long-haul? If so, bring this cycle to a close. It communicates

to your mate that you are unstable, inconsistent and indecisive.

5. Is fear and self-doubt holding you back from going to the next level in your development? If so, what steps will you commit to taking that will resolve this issue?

6. Are you a man that consistently pursues intentional growth and personal development? If not, what steps can you take to begin forming this new habit? Reading more books on a regular basis? Listening to audio courses? Enrolling in an online class?

The goal of these questions is to help you become and remain a model of your message. A physical representation of the ideas we have covered so far in this book. This philosophy is based on the leadership tactic "leading by doing" which means, intentionally becoming a visible example of a behavior you would like someone to adopt.

4 Practical ways to teach your mate

No teaching method will come close to the level of influence your life message has on others, but there are a few more teaching strategies I have found to be helpful. Some will come directly from you, while others will come from outside influences.

1. Vulnerability

Ambitious and optimistic people can mistakenly be viewed as naturally fearless and unstoppable. Open up to your mate about the reality of your fears, doubts and shortcomings. This will help reinforce the idea that these feelings are a natural part of everyone's journey.

2. Planned experiences

This can be any planned experience that helps your mate move closer to her goal. For example, my mate feels her purpose involves helping women overcome specific issues through speaking, writing books and teaching seminars. Because this is her focus, I'm always on the lookout for seminars in our area that we can attend, gatherings for women she can support, or even videos online that may be helpful to her in some way. **Once you find your mate's focus, feed it with planned experiences.**

3. A Mentor

If your mate has a goal, but is not sure how to go about implementing it, she may need a mentor. Mentors are great resources of information. With the knowledge from their experiences and mistakes, they can guide you down your chosen path more quickly and by a safer route than you could travel without them. A mentor could be an acquaintance, a professional you have to seek out or even a book (books are the most underused way to receive quality mentorship). Anyone with greater knowledge than you on a particular subject is a potential candidate for mentorship.

4. Personal growth

I've mentioned it in an earlier section, but it's worth mentioning here again; one of the most important decisions a man will ever make, is to adopt a personal growth plan.

What is a personal growth plan?

It is a purposeful plan of self-directed study, growth and development toward a desired end. This simply means that you work on becoming a better all around man by deciding what areas of your life need work and consciously choosing to tackle each area for a specified time. For years my personal plan has been aimed at incremental improvement in every major area of life: relationships, health, finances, family, mental, spiritual, and career. Create your plan based on the desired outcome you would like to achieve. Along your journey, keep this important point in mind; **while personal growth is inherently personal, it has a rippling effect on those around you. One of the best things you can do for your mate and your family as a whole, is to offer an improved you.**

▪ Points to remember ▪

1. The principle of teaching is of great importance. It is a privilege, as well as an immense responsibility of the cultivator.

2. The message you send through your life conduct is an integral component in forming an environment conducive to your mate's growth.

3. A man visibly nonchalant regarding the expression of his individual potential creates a discrepancy in his affirmation of the potential of others. However, a man whose actions match his affirmation of what's possible for others communicates believability and a feeling of inspiration that helps move them to action.

4. One of the most important decisions a man will ever make, is to adopt a personal growth plan.

CHAPTER 4

Principle #4
Love her

A flower cannot blossom without sunshine,
and man cannot live without love
— Max Muller

The final element needed to form the environment in which your mate can best succeed is love. We've talked about uncovering her purpose, encouraging her and teaching her, but loving her, is the foundational piece that holds the integrity of the environment in place. Without love, your recognition of her potential goes ignored. Without love, your encouraging words have no meaning. Without love, your teaching is rendered powerless. Doing your part to ensure the home is a place of love is an important function of being a cultivator.

The impact of love on achievement

The impact love has on achievement is often overlooked. A solid relationship anchored in love provides a psychological and emotional feeling of security that serves as a launching pad for success. When life at home is intact, it makes it easier to go out and take on the world. No problem outside the home can withstand the support and restorative power of love inside the home.

Acts of love

The concept of love has been discussed and written about for ages. Thousands of books, popular songs, poetry, and articles from leading psychologists have attempted to define it, and its many applications to life. While experts may differ on an absolute definition, we can all agree on two primary conclusions:

- The need for love is natural and universal to every human.
- Love is displayed and perpetuated through action.

The following are eight ways love can be communicated and reinforced in your relationship. Keep in mind that everyone's relationship is different. This list is in no way irrefutable. **Honor your mate's individuality by communicating with her about the unique ways she receives love and put your focus there.**

1. Maintaining an environment of openness, trust and faithfulness.

2. Learning and fulfilling her unique emotional needs, including a consistent flow of affection, intimate conversation and attention.

3. Being a pillar of stability and strength during the inevitable tough times.

4. Practicing forgiveness and understanding.

5. Consistently expressing gratitude and appreciation for both her actions, as well as her as an individual.

6. Working to resolve conflict in a reasonable and loving way.

7. Not neglecting the necessity of fun and relaxing time together.

8. Taking the time to learn how to love her through the study of literature, and most importantly, direct communication with her.

Love is built and solidified over time through commitment, not perfection. You don't need to be perfect or a relationship expert to build a loving home, but you do need to learn a few key acts of love and become diligent in their expression. This book is not meant to be a full discourse on this subject, but for further study I highly recommend three books that are considered classics:

1. *His Needs, Her Needs* by Willard Harley

2. *The Five Love Languages* by Gary Chapman

3. *Men are from Mars, Women are from Venus* by John Gray

Read these books with your mate and discuss any points that stand out along with any discrepancies you may have with the content.

▪ Points to remember ▪

1. The final element needed to form the environment in which your mate can best succeed is love.

2. Doing your part to ensure the home is a place of love is an important function of being a cultivator.

3. A solid relationship anchored in love provides a psychological and emotional feeling of security that serves as a launching pad for success.

4. Love is built and solidified over time through commitment, not perfection. You don't need be perfect or a relationship expert to build a loving home, but you do need to learn a few key acts of love and become diligent in their expression.

Conclusion

Encourage other men to cultivate

I encourage you to share this book with every man you know. This is a message that needs to read, discussed, and most of all, practiced in every home around the world. You may be thinking, "No one in my circle of friends thinks along these lines." That is good news! YOU CAN BE THE FIRST! Let the life you lead be a positive example to those in your circle of influence. Take pride in cultivating your mate and encouraging others to do the same.

Want to help me out?

Thank you for reading this book. I appreciate this investment in me more than you know. If this book has helped you in any way, please leave a review at www.amazon.com/author/mauricerogers.Thank you in advance.

Other books from the author

1. Do These Five: 5 simple tips for permanent, sustainable weight-loss.

This book covers five lifestyle changes that naturally lead to permanent, sustainable weight-loss. No gimmicks. No fad diets. No supplements to buy. Available at www.amazon.com/author/mauricerogers.

www.ingramcontent.com/pod-product-compliance
Lightning Source LLC
Chambersburg PA
CBHW071742020426
42331CB00008B/2135